Scholastic BookFiles™

A READING GUIDE TO

Sounder

by William H. Armstrong

Jeannette Sanderson

SCHOLASTIC REFERENCE

Library of Congress Cataloging-in-Publication Data
Sanderson, Jeannette.
Scholastic BookFiles: A Reading Guide to Sounder
by William H. Armstrong/by Jeannette Sanderson.
p.   cm.
Summary: Discusses the writing, characters, plot,
and themes of the Newbery Award–winning book.
Includes discussion questions and activities.
Includes bibliographical references (p.).
1. Armstrong, William Howard, 1914– . Sounder—
Juvenile literature.   2. African-American families in literature—
Juvenile literature.   3. Dogs in literature—Juvenile literature.
4. Boys in literature—Juvenile literature.   5. Poor in literature—
Juvenile literature.   [1. Armstrong, William Howard, 1914– .
Sounder.   2. American literature—History and criticism.]   I. Title.
PS3551.R483 S6837 2003
813′.54—dc21   2002191213

0-439-29797-4

10 9 8 7 6 5 4 3 2   04 05 06 07

Composition by Brad Walrod/High Text Graphics, Inc.
Cover and interior design by Red Herring Design

Printed in the U.S.A.   23
First printing, July 2003

Contents

About William H. Armstrong   5

How *Sounder* Came About   10

Chapter Charter: Questions to Guide Your Reading   12

Plot: What's Happening?   16

Setting/Time and Place: Where in the World Are We?   23

Themes/Layers of Meaning: Is That What It

   Really Means?   28

Characters: Who Are These People, Anyway?   37

Opinion: What Have Other People Thought About

   Sounder?   45

Glossary   49

William H. Armstrong on Writing   52

You Be the Author!   55

Activities   57

Related Reading   60

Bibliography   63

"To pursue excellence in whatever we do—farming, carpentry, teaching, writing (these I have done)—is to find a contentment and order in a world that seems to prefer discontent and disorder."

—William H. Armstrong

William Howard Armstrong was born on September 14, 1914, during the worst hailstorm and tornado in the memory of his Lexington, Virginia, neighbors. He was the third child born to Howard Gratton Armstrong, a farmer, and his wife, Ida Morris Armstrong. He once said of his birth, "Mother wept with joy and fear. Joy that there was a boy, a helpmate for the father on the farm after two girls. Fear for the signs—born in the midst of the destroyer of much of summer's work. What omen but bad?" Armstrong went on to defy his ominous entrance to the world, living a good, long, productive life in which he was a husband, father, teacher, farmer, carpenter, and stonemason, as well as a writer, before he died on April 11, 1999.

As he grew up, Armstrong developed a love of history. "I walked with history," he said. "Lexington and Rockbridge

County [Virginia,] were living history. George Washington had carved his initials high on Natural Bridge. [Texas freedom fighter] Sam Houston had been born here. . . . My grandfather had ridden with [Confederate general Stonewall] Jackson. . . . Little wonder that my favorite subject . . . was history."

But school was not easy for Armstrong. In fact, in the early grades he hated school. "I was . . . quite miserable during the early years of school," he said. "Suffering from chronic asthma, I was never picked for a team on the playground at recess. I was a runt and the only boy in school who wore glasses." To make matters worse, he developed a stutter after finding his favorite pony kicked to death by horses.

What changed Armstrong's life? A teacher.

"In sixth grade my life changed in a single day," Armstrong recalled. His teacher, Mrs. Parker, held up his homework paper for all to see and announced, "William Armstrong has the neatest paper in the class." Armstrong felt like a different person. "For the first time in my life, someone had called my name as a winner. . . . That day began a Depression-born country boy's determined journey toward 'the gates of excellence,' . . . accepting one's lot and doing one's best at it."

Growing up on a farm also taught Armstrong many valuable lessons that he carried through his life. Helping with farm chores taught him the value of work and discipline. Armstrong later said, "What a glorious thing for my future that my father taught me to work."

These lessons helped him finish school during the Great Depression, when so many others dropped out. The Great Depression of the 1930s was a long and harsh economic slump that left millions of people unemployed. During the Depression, many banks and other businesses failed, and as a result, many people lost their jobs, their money that had been in saving accounts, and their homes because they could not pay a mortgage. Conditions were so harsh that in 1932, at least 25,000 families and 200,000 young people wandered the country looking for food to eat, a place to live, and a job. By studying and working hard through these trying times, Armstrong managed to finish school.

While his father taught him to work hard, his mother taught Armstrong to love stories. Ida Armstrong read the Bible to her children every day. "No one told me the Bible was not for young readers, so I found some exciting stories in it," Armstrong said. "Not until years later did I understand why I liked the Bible stories so much. It was because everything that could possibly be omitted [left out] was omitted. There was no description of David so I could be like David. Ahab and Naboth were just like some people down the road." Armstrong later used the art of omission in his own writing of *Sounder.*

Armstrong went on to excel in high school and college. He attended Hampden-Sydney College in Prince Edward Island County, Virginia. Armstrong wrote for the college's newspaper and its literary magazine, and even served as the magazine's editor. When he graduated from Hampden-Sydney College in 1936, he considered a career in journalism. But another teacher,

Dr. David C. Wilson at Hampden-Sydney, inspired Armstrong to teach. "Perhaps the wisest decision I ever made," Armstrong later said.

After his college graduation, Armstrong taught at an Episcopal school in Lynchburg, Virginia. As he settled into his career, he also became settled in his family life. In 1943, William Howard Armstrong married Martha Stone Street. The following year, the couple moved to Kent, Connecticut, where Armstrong took a position teaching general studies and ancient history to ninth-grade boys at Kent School.

Nine years later, Martha Armstrong died suddenly, leaving her husband and three young children, ages four, six, and eight. "Without even the aid of a housekeeper, we managed," Armstrong said. "We have grown up together."

The values of work and discipline that he had learned at an early age helped William Armstrong accomplish a great deal. They helped him clear a rocky hillside and build a house with his own hands. They helped him with the difficult job of raising three young children after his wife's sudden death. And they helped him find time to write while teaching full-time and raising his young sons and daughter.

Armstrong taught at Kent School for fifty-two years. Early in his career there, the headmaster urged him to write a book about how to study, telling Armstrong that he had "the best organized, best disciplined, best prepared students in the school." That suggestion resulted in Armstrong's first book, *Study Is Hard*

Work, published in 1956. Armstrong went on to write more than fifteen books on a wide variety of subjects. The best known of these is the 1969 classic, *Sounder,* which he wrote based on an account told around his family's kitchen table in Virginia.

Despite the number of books he wrote, Armstrong did not think of himself as a writer. "I'm a teacher," he said. And, as with everything he did, Armstrong pursued excellence in this career. "Teaching is more than the subject and the textbook," he once said. "It's hopefully directing some young wanderer in a direction that will add quality, and, in rare cases, love of learning to a life."

One of the things Armstrong taught his students was that "time is the most limited blessing that we have upon this earth." Armstrong made the most of his eighty-five years. Readers may remember him for *Sounder,* but Armstrong saw his contributions differently. "After teaching, building an uncoursed stone wall to stand as long as time gives me greatest pleasure."

Armstrong died at his home in Kent, Connecticut, on April 11, 1999, but *Sounder,* the book he wrote more than thirty years earlier, continues to be read all over the world.

How *Sounder* Came About

"The fragment of a memory from a
story told me by a black man started
the mystery of his childhood in my
mind."

—William H. Armstrong

In his Author's Note at the beginning of *Sounder*, William Armstrong describes sitting around his family's kitchen table when he was a child and listening to a gray-haired black man tell stories from Aesop, the Old Testament, Homer, and history. The man was the teacher in the one-room school for black children several miles from Armstrong's home, and he worked for Armstrong's father after school and in the summer. One night, he told a story from Homer's epic poem, the *Odyssey.* The tale was about Argus, Odysseus's faithful dog, who recognized his master when he returned home after being away for twenty years. Then the man told the story of his own faithful dog. That dog was Sounder.

"It was history—*his* history," Armstrong wrote. And this history so captured Armstrong's heart and mind that fifty years later, while walking along the Housatonic River in Connecticut one October evening, he imagined he heard the dog's bark. About that night, Armstrong wrote, "Was the October night's song lasting enough to let a lone walker's ears pick up the faint, distant voice of Sounder, the great coon dog, a voice the stroller in the night had never heard, but had only heard about, so many years ago from a black man?" The answer was yes.

Armstrong began to think again about the man who had told the story, about "the mystery of his childhood." He began to ask himself, "How did he achieve such excellence? What, against all odds, in a world of neglect, hurt, oppression, and loneliness kept the desire to learn alive in him? That, long after he was dead, would be my story. I would create his boyhood with that desire to learn, supported by love and self-respect, which produced the remarkable man."

That night, Armstrong said he knew "I must use this memory. I must write *Sounder.* But not yet. Autumn is too beautiful. It must wait for winter. . . . And when in winter? Not in the quiet peace of evening, but the cold dark of early morning, with anxious glances toward the mountain beyond the river to see if a dawn will ever break, but knowing that it will."

Armstrong wrote the book that winter. In fact, he wrote a trilogy. When he showed the long manuscript to a neighbor who was a book reviewer, the man suggested he break up the manuscript into three books. These became *Sounder* and its sequels, *The Sour Land*, and *The MacLeod Place*.

The following questions will help you think about the important parts of each chapter.

Chapter 1

- Why do you think the boy is so fond of Sounder? Have you ever felt that way about an animal?
- Do you think Sounder is a good name for the dog? Can you think of any other names that might have suited him?
- What kind of life do the boy and his family have? Do you think it would be easy or difficult for them to change their life? Why?
- The author says that in winter, there are no crops and no pay. What do you think are some of the challenges of raising a family without a regular source of income?
- Where do you think the father got the sausage and hambone? How can you tell that both the father and the mother are worried about something?
- Why is it so important to the boy that he learn to read?

Chapter 2

- What do you think of the sheriff and his deputies? Do you think they are fair law-enforcers?
- Why do you think the father leaves with the sheriff without a fight?
- What does it say about how white people treated black people in this time and place when a deputy calls the father "boy"?

- Do you think the father can expect a fair trial?
- Why does the mother seem so calm in the face of such troubles?
- What do you think is going to happen to the boy's father?
- Do you think Sounder will survive?

Chapter 3

- Why does the boy's mother return the pork sausage and ham? Do you think it will do the father any good?
- One hymn the boy's mother often sings or hums has these lines: "You gotta walk that lonesome valley, You gotta walk it by yourself, Ain't nobody else gonna walk it for you." How do you think this hymn relates to her life?
- What do you think happened to Sounder? Where is his body?

Chapter 4

- Do you think the mother should have given back the sausages and ham? Why or why not?
- The mother tells the boy that he must learn to lose. She says, "Some people is born to keep. Some is born to lose. We was born to lose, I reckon." Do you agree with her? Do you think there's anything she can do to change that?
- Do you think the boy is right to be afraid going into town? Why or why not?
- Were you surprised at how the jailer treats the boy and the cake?
- The boy deals with his hatred for the jailer by imagining him choking himself to death as he had seen a bull once do. Do you think it's helpful or harmful for the boy to have such thoughts? What would you do if you were in his position?

Chapter 5

- How does the boy's Christmas compare with the holiday as it is probably being celebrated in most of the big houses in town?
- Why do you think the boy's mother is kind and gentle to him when he returns from the jail?
- Why do you think Sounder no longer barks?
- Do you think the punishment of hard labor fits the father's crime of stealing the ham and sausage? Do you think he got a fair trial? Do you think there are ever circumstances when stealing would be okay?

Chapter 6

- Why do you think the boy doesn't remember his age? What helps you remember your age?
- Do you think the boy should listen to his mother and just wait for his father to come home, or should he go out looking for him? What would you have done?
- How is the boy usually treated when he searches for his father? Why do you think he keeps searching?
- What is the one good thing about the boy's search for his father?
- Why are stories so important to the boy? How does remembering them help him during his search?

Chapter 7

- The mother says to the boy, "There's patience, child, and waitin' that's got to be." Do you think she's right to be patient? Does she have a choice?
- The boy imagines that, had he been there, his father would have attacked the guard who threw a piece of iron at him. Do you agree? Why or why not?

- The boy fantasizes about throwing a piece of iron at the guard and killing him. Why do you think he doesn't do this?
- When the boy finds a book, he reads a section called Cruelty. How do these words relate to the boy's life (even though he doesn't yet understand what they say)?
- Why is the boy sure that the plant the man worries over must be something to eat? Up until now, do you think the boy has often—or ever—been able to enjoy something just for its beauty?
- Do you think this man will help the boy? If so, how?

Chapter 8
- Do you think the mother is right to let the boy go live with the teacher? Is the boy right to go? Why or why not?
- After the boy reads to his brother and sisters, the mother says, "The Lord has come to you, child." Why do you think she says that?
- Why doesn't the boy tell his mother what the term "dog days" really means?
- Even before they know the figure they see coming is the father, why do the boy and his mother suspect it is him?
- What does it say about the father that, despite his enormous injuries, he manages to make it home?
- Why do you think the boy and the mother aren't sadder when the father dies?
- The boy had read in his book, "Only the unwise think that what has changed is dead." What does that mean? How does this thought console him now? Do you have a memory of someone or something that comforts you when you think of it?

"Maybe his father didn't know Sounder was dead. Maybe his father was dead in the back of the sheriff's wagon now."

—*Sounder*

Sounder is the story of a poor black sharecropper (see page 24) who is arrested for stealing food and how his family—especially his older son—deals with his absence, as well as with the shooting of their beloved dog, Sounder.

The story starts with the father and son standing on the front porch of their cabin one October evening with their coon dog, Sounder. The father tells his son that if the wind does not rise, they will go hunting together that night. Farming season is over, and with no crops there is no pay. A possum or coon hide would bring in much-needed money to help pay for food and warm clothes.

The boy loves to hunt with his father and Sounder. The dog has a voice like no other's. Sounder is the boy's consolation for not being able to go to school. He has tried, but the eight-mile trip is too far to make twice a day. One day, he tells himself, he will go to school. In the meantime, he has Sounder.

When the boy and his father go into the cabin, the boy eats with his younger sisters and brother while his mother and father talk about how poor the crop was this year and how bad the hunting has been.

After supper, the father goes out alone. The boy wonders where his father has gone without Sounder; they always go out together at night.

After the father leaves, the mother sits in her rocker picking walnut meat, called kernels, out of their shells to bring to the store to sell. The boy asks his mother to tell him one of her Bible stories, which help chase away his loneliness.

The next morning, the boy awakes to the smell of pork sausages and ham cooking. His mother is humming and her lips are rolled inward—both signs that she's worried—but the boy barely notices, he's so happy to be filling his stomach with good food, so glad to be able to give Sounder more than scraps to eat.

That night his mother does not tell stories or sing; she hums "That Lonesome Road" while she picks walnut kernels. The boy feels very lonely. He vows, "One day I will learn to read" to keep from feeling lonely.

Three days later, the white sheriff and his deputies arrive. They push themselves into the house and roughly handcuff the boy's father while the family, frozen in terror, looks on.

Suddenly Sounder, who has been out in the fields, is growling and scratching at the door. One of the deputies pushes the boy outside, telling him, "Get that dog out of the way and hold him if you don't want him dead."

The boy tries to hold Sounder as the sheriff and his men put chains on his father and push him into the back of a wagon. Sounder breaks free of the boy's grasp, chasing the wagon as it is pulled away. One of the deputies turns and shoots the dog. The boy's father does not even lift his head to look as Sounder falls in the road, the whole side of his head and shoulder torn off.

Sounder is not dead, though. He manages to drag himself under the porch. The next morning, the boy's mother takes the walnut kernels to the store to sell them. She also takes the remaining sausage and ham with her.

The boy crawls under the cabin and looks for Sounder. He is not there. He looks along the road the way the wagon went and searches the entire area around the cabin. The dog is nowhere to be found. When his mother returns, she tells the boy that maybe Sounder went off to die, or maybe he went into the woods to try to heal his wounds with oak leaves. But she warns him, "Don't be all hope, child."

Weeks go by and the boy searches everywhere for the dog; he cannot find him.

Christmas comes and the mother bakes a big cake for the father, and asks the boy to bring it to him at the jail. The jailer is a cruel man. He tears apart the cake, then makes the boy clean up the mess. When the boy gets to see his father, both man and child are so sad they hardly know what to say to each other.

The next morning, Sounder comes home. He is in bad shape: "One front foot dangled above the floor. The stub of an ear stuck out on one side, and there was no eye on that side." But he is alive. He wags his tail and licks the boy's hand. He does not bark, however. The only sound he makes is a whine.

A short while later, his mother gets word that his father has been sentenced to hard labor.

Now "loneliness put its stamp on everything." And just as the family's loneliness increases, so does its hardship. The mother takes in more washing. The boy, though young, goes out to work in the fields.

As the boy grows, he becomes restless and wants to find his father. He searches for him in autumn, when the fieldwork is through. Though he visits many road camps, prison farms, and stone quarries, he never finds his father. These journeys are difficult, and the boy tries to keep up his courage and keep away loneliness by remembering the Bible stories his mother has told him.

During one journey, the boy is hurt when a guard at a road camp throws a piece of iron at him that hits his hand. The day is not all bad, however. The boy later finds a book someone has thrown in the trash. Though he cannot read well, he is happy to have a book of his own.

The boy stops at a small water pump next to a school for black children to clean his wound, and the teacher there takes him home to wash it in warm soapy water. The boy has trouble believing what he sees in the man's cabin. The man grows flowers, he has two lamps, and there are shelves and shelves of books. The man tells the boy a story from the book the boy found. The boy tells the man about his father and about Sounder.

When the boy returns home, his mother sees that he is excited. She thinks that he has found his father, but the boy says no, and tells his mother about the teacher. He tells her that the teacher has asked him to go back to him and go to school, to live in the teacher's cabin and do his chores. "Go child," the mother says. "The Lord has come to you."

The boy goes to school in fall and winter and spring, but comes home in summer to take his father's place in the fields, to pay the rent. Sounder always greets him by wagging his tail and whining, but he never barks.

One hot August day, six years after his father had been sent away, the boy and his mother are sitting on a shaded corner of the porch. Sounder is acting strangely, and his mother attributes it to the heat.

As they sit, a speck appears in the distance. They can't make out if it's a person or an animal. Sounder is increasingly agitated as the figure approaches, then he lets out the first bark that they've heard in six years and runs off down the road.

It is the father. He had been caught in a dynamite blast in the prison quarry, and half of his body had been crushed by limestone. The doctors had been sure he was going to die, but the man was determined to go home.

Summer turns into autumn and the boy goes back to school. He comes home in October to help gather wood and walnuts for the winter. His father, remembering Octobers past, decides to go hunting. He and Sounder set off with the lantern as they had hundreds of times before.

Just before dawn, Sounder comes home alone. He leads the boy back into the woods, where he finds his father, leaning against a tree, the lantern still burning at his side. He is dead. The boy goes home and tells his mother. She is sad, but happy, too. "When life is tiresome," she says, "there ain't no peace like the greatest peace—the peace of the Lord's hand holding you."

After they bury his father, it is time for the boy to go back to school again. But before he leaves, he digs a grave for Sounder. He "ain't got no spirit left for living," the boy tells his mother.

"He'll be gone before I come home again." Sounder dies two weeks before the boy comes home for Christmas.

The boy consoles himself by remembering a line from the book he'd found years ago, which he can now read as well as understand. "Only the unwise think that what has changed is dead." The boy knows that his father and Sounder will live forever in his memory, like "a lantern burning out of oil but not going out."

Thinking about the plot
• Why does the boy's father steal the food? Do you think he has a choice?
• How is the boy finally able to make his life better?
• How does the boy choose to remember his father and Sounder? Why?

"The white man who owned the vast endless fields had scattered the cabins of his Negro sharecroppers far apart, like flyspecks on a whitewashed ceiling."

—Sounder

Sounder takes place in the rural South around the beginning of the twentieth century. There are no place-names and no dates. Throughout the book, Armstrong practices the "art of omission," leaving out specific details that might limit the ability of readers to place themselves in the book.

Although the author leaves out many details, he does give enough for the reader to get a general feel for where the story is taking place. From the descriptions of the land—the foothills and the flatlands, the pine woods and lowlands—we can infer, or make an educated guess, that we are in the southern United States. This is where much of the sharecropping took place after the Civil War. The weather also helps place the story there: It is very hot in the summer, and though it is cold in the winter, there is no snow.

Other details provide clues for when the story is taking place. We can assume that it takes place after the Civil War because the family in *Sounder* are sharecroppers, as are the black families that live in the cabins that surround them, and sharecroppers generally took the place of slaves on large farms and plantations after the Civil War. It is probably a fair amount of time after the Civil War, too, as there is no mention of war or slavery. The story is not too recent, however, as sharecropping became increasingly unpopular in the United States in the early twentieth century. Another clue about the time of the story is the fact that the sheriff and his deputies do not come to arrest the father in a patrol car, but on horseback and with a horse-drawn wagon.

We feel the poverty, desolation, and isolation of this family's world from the very beginning of the book. We feel their poverty when they say, "The crop will be better next year. There'll be more day work. The hunting was better last year." We feel it when we learn that the people, as well as the dog, are hungry, that "corn mush had to take the place of stewed possum, dumplings, and potatoes." And we feel it when we see the father risk his life and his family's livelihood to steal food to fill their empty stomachs.

Under the sharecropping system, a family rented a section of a large farm, which they would pay for with a portion of the crops they raised. The sharecropping families were always poor and often, though not always, black. Because they were poor, they seldom had the money they needed to buy seeds and fertilizer, and would have to get these from the landowner. As a result, by the time the sharecroppers harvested their crop, they owed money to the landowner for rent and supplies and, sometimes, equipment rental. This often meant the sharecropper had barely enough money to feed his family, if there was any money left at all. There was usually not enough money leftover to buy supplies for next year, so the cycle continued. The poor sharecroppers were always indebted to the wealthy white landowners.

Armstrong also provides many details to give the reader a strong sense of the family's isolation. "No dim light from the other cabins punctuated the night," Armstrong writes, then describes how spread out the cabins are. Even the schoolhouse is on the edge of town, eight miles away, removing the children's chance of getting an education, isolating them even more.

Once in a while, the family visits other families in the "distant cabins," or goes to the meetinghouse, but this happens so rarely that we never see it. As for visitors to the cabin, "Almost no one passed on the road in winter. . . . Even in summer a speck on the horizon was a curiosity." The only time that we see outsiders come to the cabin is when the sheriff and his deputies come to arrest the father.

The setting is desolate as well. The boy describes what he sees when he looks out the window: "Nothing moved except what the wind moved—dead leaves under the cabin, brown blades and stalks from the fields which were dead and ready to be blown away, bare branches of poplars, and the spires of tall pines."

Armstrong also makes us feel the fear, ignorance, and prejudice of the time and place. Fear seems to be a constant in this family's life. There's the fear of going hungry, but even greater is the fear of what white people can do to them. We start to feel that fear after the father brings home the sausage and ham. We feel it when the sheriff and his deputies push their way into the house and the family freezes, no one in the family speaks, no one moves. We feel the fear when the father is hit in the face with the chain and when Sounder is shot. We feel the boy's fear when he goes to see his father on Christmas and is afraid he will be stopped on the way to town. We feel the fear when the jailer destroys the cake and makes the boy clean up the mess. And we are reminded of that fear when the boy's mother tells him, "Be careful what you carry off, child. It can cause a heap o' trouble."

The lack of education of the time is shown in several ways. First, there are the many people—represented by the mother and father—who cannot read and write. A large part of the population lives in ignorance since they have very few opportunities to get an education.

Ignorance is also shown in the hateful and hurtful racial prejudice of that time and place. This prejudice is found throughout the book, especially when the reader looks closely at the sharecropping system. This black family, like many sharecroppers, works hard but is stuck in poverty, while the white landowner reaps the wealth. There is also the prejudice that limits a black person's education—does not even allow it— by making schools hard to get to. And even when the school is not far away, there is often so much work that the children cannot be spared from the fields to go to school. There is the prejudice that sentences a father to years of hard labor for stealing food to try to feed his family, when food could not be got in any other way.

There are also the physical and verbal abuses of prejudice. The sheriff calls the father "boy," and at first the elder son thinks the sheriff must be talking to him. By refusing to address the father as a man, especially in front of his wife and children, the sheriff shows him no respect. The father is chained and pushed into the back of a wagon. It's no better in jail, where the jailer destroys the father's Christmas cake and pushes the boy out at the end of visiting hours.

Thinking about the setting

- Can you imagine living in the time and place described in *Sounder*?
- How do you think you could survive living in that time and place?
- How could education have helped the boy and his family overcome their poverty?

"Some people is born to keep. Some is born to lose. We was born to lose, I reckon."

—Mother, *Sounder*

Loss

Sounder is a story of seemingly overwhelming loss. The theme of loss is threaded throughout the book. First, the family loses the father—and main source of income—when he is dragged off by the sheriff and his deputies for stealing food so that his family can eat. Then they nearly lose their pet and hunting dog, Sounder, when one of the deputies shoots him in the head and the dog drags himself off to heal or to die, no one knows which.

When the boy keeps looking for the dog, his mother tells him, "Sounder might come home again. But you must learn to lose, child. The Lord teaches the old to lose. The young don't know how to learn it."

Sounder does come back, very badly injured though alive. That does little to make up for the loss of the father when he is sentenced to hard labor. His family does not know where he will be sent or when he will be back.

When the boy loses his father, he loses his childhood, or what little of it he had. In addition to doing his regular chores, he now has to go into the fields in place of his father: The rent still has to be paid, the family still has to eat. He also works to help his mother in her efforts to make more money.

Besides being asked to work like a man, the boy must now look at the world like a man. His belief in the strength of his father is shattered with his father's arrest. He watches the white men treat his father like a child, or an animal, and sees that his father has no power or authority to resist them. When Sounder is shot and his father does not even look to see what happened, the boy sees a different man from the one who could lift a hot pot lid with his bare hands, a different man from the one who often took the lantern and went off hunting with the dog.

The loss does not end there. The father returns home severely disabled: One side of his body was crushed in a dynamite blast at the prison quarry. After the father is home for several months, he decides to go hunting with Sounder. When Sounder comes home alone, the boy follows the dog back into the woods, where he finds his father leaning against a tree trunk, dead. Sounder dies a short while later.

Courage

Courage is another important theme in *Sounder*. Despite losing a loved one, the boy and his family never give up. Their courage always gives them strength to face another day.

The mother shows this courage when she goes to town to return the uneaten ham and sausages. People will probably be mean to her in town, but she goes anyway, because it might help her husband. She hums a song as she leaves, one that seems to give her the courage she needs throughout the story:

> *You gotta walk that lonesome valley,*
> *You gotta walk it by yourself,*
> *Ain't nobody else gonna walk it for you.*

The boy shows his courage when he does all that needs to be done, despite his fears. He is very frightened walking into town to visit his father in jail on Christmas Day, but he doesn't think to say no when his mother tells him he must go. When he goes to work in the fields, he is younger than the other workers, and is "afraid and lonely." But he knows that he must work in his father's place.

The boy also displays courage when he goes out searching for his father. He is very much alone in his search, and people are often cruel to him, but he keeps looking. Even when he is hurt one day outside a road camp after a guard throws a piece of iron at him, the boy "had not run but stood still and defiant, sucking the blood from his bruised fingers." As afraid as he is—and

Armstrong tells us that the boy is always afraid when he is away from home—he keeps looking for his father.

One of the ways the father shows his great strength and courage is by dragging himself home from the prison quarry where he was badly injured in a dynamite blast. The doctors had told him he would die, but "he would not die, even with a half-dead body, because he wanted to come home again."

Family

The father's determination to return home is an example of how important family is in Sounder. Although the author hints at other relationships that his characters have—with other sharecroppers, with people at church, with the people for whom the family works—their most important relationships are with one another. The people in this family live in a very isolated world, and a cruel one, too, so they must rely on one another for support as well as companionship.

Loyalty

The theme of loyalty runs throughout Sounder. The family members show great loyalty to one another and to Sounder, and the dog shows great loyalty to them all, especially to the father, his master.

There are countless ways the family members show their loyalty: The mother does not say anything about the father stealing the food, because she knows that he did it only to feed his family.

The boy, knowing his mother has probably had a hard day in town, tells his siblings not to bother her when she comes home after returning the ham and sausages. "She won't bring no stick candy," he tells them. "Don't ask her for none. Don't ask her nothin'." When the mother sends the boy to bring the father a cake for Christmas, she tells her son, "Whatever you do, child, act perkish and don't grieve your father." At the jail, the father tells the boy to tell the mother not to grieve and not to send the boy anymore. And the boy decides to hide the harsh truth of the jail from his mother.

The boy shows his loyalty to Sounder by making sure the dog has enough to eat; after his father steals the ham and sausages, the boy says, "Sounder will eat good now." The boy also proves his loyalty to the dog by searching far and wide for him after he is hurt.

Examples of Sounder's loyalty include when he growls and scratches at the door when the sheriff and his deputies are in the cabin. He chases after them and is shot while doing so. He drags himself to the woods to heal himself, then comes home. While he is devoted to all the family, his deepest loyalty is to his master. "Whether he lay in the sun on the cabin porch or by the side of the road, the one eye was always turned in the direction his master had gone."

While his master is away, Sounder's famous voice is silenced. Then his master comes home and Sounder is the first to recognize him: He is "a young dog again. His voice was the same mellow sound that had ridden the November breeze from the lowlands to the hills." Sounder goes hunting one last time with his master, then runs home to get the boy when the man dies in the woods. After that, the boy tells his mother, "Sounder ain't got no spirit left for living. He hasn't gone with me to the woods to chop since Pa died. He doesn't even whine anymore." Sounder lives to see his master come home; two months after his master dies, Sounder dies, too.

Racial injustice

Sounder tries to protect his family against the white sheriff and his deputies, but it is a losing battle: There is no way to protect the family against racial injustice. Struggling to maintain dignity in the face of prejudice is a major theme in this book. Armstrong shows us a world in which a hardworking father, forced to steal so that his family does not go hungry, is given such a harsh punishment that it eventually kills him. He shows us a world where black people cannot fight back, are afraid to walk down the street, and are sent to the back doors of the white men's houses. And he shows us a world where the only hope, the only way out—education—is often denied to black people.

Importance of education

The boy desperately wants an education and is determined to get it. This leads to another significant theme in *Sounder:* the importance of education.

There is so much that the family is unable to do because none of them can read or write. The family cannot write letters to one another when they are separated; the mother cannot write to the judge, asking him not to be harsh in sentencing the father; she cannot read the newspaper to find out when the father is sentenced, but must rely on others to do it for her.

The boy wants to learn to read, but not because he thinks education will lead to a different life. He thinks of it as a way to make the life he lives more bearable. He says to himself, "One day I will learn to read." He wants "a book with stories in it, then he wouldn't be lonesome even if his mother didn't sing."

When the boy meets the teacher who befriends him, he realizes that an education *can* also lead to a much different life. The boy is amazed when he is in the teacher's cabin: It "had two lamps, both lit at the same time, and two stoves, one to cook on and one to warm by. . . . and there were shelves filled not with pans and dishes, but with books." These are luxuries not found in the boy's home or in the homes of other sharecroppers.

When the boy tells his mother that the teacher wants him to come and stay with him so he can go to school, the mother lets him go, even though it will cause some hardship for her. "It's a sign," she says. "The Lord has come to you." She understands the importance of education.

Personal growth

Personal growth is another theme in *Sounder*, and book learning is just one of the ways the boy grows.

At the beginning of the story, the author shows us a boy whose only wishes are to go hunting with his father and to learn to read. When the story ends six years later, we see a boy who has learned to do a man's work. We see a boy whose father returns severely disabled and accepts it. While his mother sits "suffocated in shock," the boy says to his father in a clear voice, "Sounder knew it was you just like you was comin' home from work." He even knows enough to go around the cabin and warn his younger siblings about their father's appearance. "Pa's home," he says. "He's mighty crippled up, so behave like nothin' has happened."

We also see a boy who has come to understand the meaning of the words "Only the unwise think that what has changed is dead." When he first reads these words in the book he has found, he doesn't understand them. His teacher explains their meaning: "If a flower blooms once, it goes on blooming somewhere forever. It blooms on for whoever has seen it blooming." Even then, the boy doesn't understand him. But as he grows, he comes to understand the meaning of the words. So when he thinks of his father and Sounder, it isn't as how they were when they died. He remembers them at their best: "The pine trees would look down forever on a lantern burning out of oil but not going out. A harvest moon would cast shadows forever of a man walking upright, his dog bouncing after him."

Hope

Finally, *Sounder* is about hope, and that is a theme of great importance in the book. There is hope in this family, and that is how they survive. By not giving up, the boy is able to get an education. Despite all the difficulties in his life—the fear, ignorance, and prejudice of the time and place—there is hope for the future.

<table>
<tr><td colspan="1">

Thinking about the themes

• What do you think is the most important theme in *Sounder*?

• Can you imagine continuing on in the face of so much loss? How would you do it? How do the boy and his family do it?

• Why does the boy want to learn to read? Why is reading important to you?

• How does the boy remember his father and Sounder?

</td></tr>
</table>

Characters: Who Are These People, Anyway?

The four main characters in this book are the boy, the father, the mother, and the coon dog, Sounder. Other characters include the boy's brother and sisters, the sheriff and his deputies, the jailer, the road camp guard, and the teacher.

Here is a list of characters. Following that is a brief description of the main characters.

boy	the oldest child in the sharecropper's family
father	a sharecropper
mother	the sharecropper's wife
Sounder	the family's pet and hunting dog
brother and sisters	younger children in the sharecropper's family
sheriff and deputies	the men who arrest the father
jailer	the man who keeps watch at the father's jail
road camp guard	a guard at one of the prison road camps
teacher	the man who helps the boy get in school

Boy: The boy—who, like the other human characters in the story, is nameless—is the main character in *Sounder*. Armstrong never tells us the boy's age. Even the boy does not know it; all he knows is that he has "lived a long, long time." Based on the fact that he is allowed to hunt with his father and does a man's work after his father is in jail, we can guess that the boy is somewhere around ten or eleven years old. During the course of the book, we see the boy suffer great loss, we see him take on many challenges, and we see him grow up.

At the start of the story, the boy wants to go hunting with his father. It is clear that he admires his father and that he adores the family's dog, Sounder. The boy loves him so much that he consoles himself with the fact that if he can't have an education, at least he can have Sounder.

The boy desperately wants to go to school. For the past two years he has tried to walk the eight miles each way to and from school, but it has been too far. He gets there late, and the other children make fun of him. When it turns cold and his mother tells him to give up, he does, vowing to try again next year, when he is bigger, stronger, and faster.

The main reason the boy wants to go to school is to learn to read. He is lonely and finds comfort in the Bible stories his mother tells him and in the songs that she sings. But sometimes his mother doesn't want to tell stories or sing. The boy thinks that one day he will learn to read. "Then he wouldn't be lonesome even if his mother didn't sing."

The boy loves his father and is very proud of him. He sees him as strong and brave, as a fighter. The boy's image of his father is destroyed, however, when the sheriff and his deputies come and arrest him. They call the father "boy," they chain him up, and he does not resist. Later, the boy must struggle with feelings of pity and anger when he sees his father in jail.

Because he loves him, the boy worries about his father. He worries about how cold he is in the back of the wagon in his torn overalls. He worries about how warm it is in jail. He worries about how he will keep in touch—since no one in the family can read or write—while he is in prison and at the labor camp.

The boy is thoughtful and considerate of his mother. When she goes to town to sell walnuts as well as to return the stolen ham and sausages after his father's arrest, he knows the people will be mean to her. When he sees her coming back down the road, he tells his younger siblings not to bother her when she returns. He is quiet when he sees that "her eyes were filled with hurt."

The boy is forced to grow up quickly in his father's absence. In addition to worrying about his parents, he must do more work to help pay the rent and buy food for the family. He helps his mother string more clotheslines for the laundry, does "yard work at the big houses where he had gathered weeds behind his father," and goes out to work in the fields. He does so without complaint, despite the fact that he is lonely and afraid.

The boy is also very loyal. He is loyal to the dog he loves after the animal is shot in the road. He leaves food for him. He crawls under the house looking for him. He sleeps with Sounder's ear under his pillow, willing the dog to survive. When the dog disappears, he searches high and low for him and always waits for his return.

The boy also searches for his father. The searching is hard: He is lonely in his travels, and when he does meet people, they are often cruel to him.

Despite the hard work and the disappointments, the boy keeps one hope very much alive: to learn to read. And his journeys do accomplish "one wonderful thing. In the towns . . . people threw newspapers and magazines into trash barrels, . . . so he could always find something with which to practice his reading." Then, one day, he finds something even better: a book. "All his life he had wanted a book."

Although it takes many years to happen, the boy learns to read. Because of this ability, he is able to turn to words from the book he found to help him deal with the deaths of his father and Sounder. The boy, now a man, knows that though his father and Sounder may be buried under the cold, hard earth, they will live on in his memory forever.

Father: The father is another important character in this book. He is tall and strong and protective of his family. Though he doesn't say it, his actions prove how much he loves his family, his home, and his dog, Sounder.

The author describes the father's hands: "hands that could handle a pot lid without a pot rag, open the stove door without a poker, or skin a possum by holding the hind legs of the carcass with one hand and the hide with the other and just pulling." But these are the same hands that come forward when the sheriff takes out his handcuffs and says, "Stick out your hands, boy."

The father is strong, but he knows that there are some fights that he cannot win.

Before he is arrested, the father tries to win the fight against hunger. He works hard in the fields, he does yard work at the big houses, and he goes hunting. But when the crops are poor and the hunting is bad, there isn't enough food. So the man goes out one night and steals a ham and some pork sausages from the smokehouse. His protectiveness gets his family three days of good eating; it also gets him sentenced to many years of hard labor.

The father shows how much he loves his family in many ways besides working hard and stealing for them. When the boy comes to visit him in jail at Christmas, he sends him home to tell his mother he'll be back before long, "tell her not to grieve," and "tell her not to send you no more."

He expresses his love for his dog by putting burlap sacks under the porch so that the dog is warm when the frosts come; he tells his wife to "save the ham-boilin' for Sounder."

In the end, after he is very badly wounded in a dynamite blast at the prison quarry, the father shows the strength of his love and his determination when he refuses to die and manages to drag his injured body home.

Mother: The mother, another major character in the book, accepts whatever bad happens in her life as if it were meant to be. She has a strong belief in God. She is patient and stern and, in her own way, loving. She is also a hard worker.

The mother demonstrates her acceptance of her harsh life in many ways. After the father is arrested and Sounder is shot, she does not break down and cry. She simply calls the boy into the house. "Come in, child," she says, "and bring some wood." Later, when the boy cannot find Sounder, the mother urges him to accept the loss of his beloved pet. And when the boy searches and searches but cannot find his father, she says, "It's all powerful puzzlin' and aggravatin', but it's the Lord's will."

The mother believes that much of what happens, bad as well as good, is "the Lord's will." When the boy tells her that the teacher wants him to come back and go to school, the mother says, "Go, child. The Lord has come to you." And when the father dies, the mother is only momentarily sad. "When life is so tiresome, there ain't no peace like the greatest peace—the peace of the Lord's hand holding you."

The mother declares her spirituality in the songs she sings and the stories she tells. She hums and sings spirituals—black religious folk songs—to get her through good times and bad. She also tells stories from the Bible that she has heard at the meetinghouse.

The mother's patience is revealed when she is speaking to the boy. "Don't fret," she says when the boy becomes anxious to go looking for his father. "Time's passin'. Won't be much longer now." Later, after he returns from one of his many fruitless searches, she tells the boy, "There's patience, child, and waitin' that's got to be."

We see how stern the mother is when the boy reaches for a walnut from the pile in her lap, and she slaps his hand. "You eat the crumbs from the bottom of the hull basket," she says. While that sounds cruel, it's simply what she has to do to make enough money to feed the family. "I try to pick two pounds a night," she says. "That's thirty cents' worth."

It is clear, however, that the mother wants the boy to have more than crumbs. She washes his pillowcase and sheet every week, just like she does "for the people who [live] in the big house down the road." When the boy comes in after not finding Sounder, she says, "You're tired and worried poorly," and gives him the icing pan to lick.

She shows her love to her husband by trying to keep the house quiet so that he can sleep the morning after he steals the ham and sausages. And she bakes him a cake for Christmas that is three times bigger than the one she keeps for the rest of the family.

Like the father, the mother is a hard worker. She does laundry for the people who live in the big houses, and after her husband is arrested, she stretches longer clotheslines and does more of it. She also picks walnut kernels to try to make extra money.

Sounder: The dog, because of the loyalty he shows his master and his family, is a main character in the book. Sounder, a cross between a Georgia redbone hound and a bulldog, got his name because of his voice. The author writes that "no price . . . could be put on Sounder's voice. It came out of the great chest cavity and broad jaws as though it had bounced off the walls of a cave. It mellowed into half-echo before it touched the air. . . . it was not an ordinary bark. It filled up the night and made music as though the branches of all the trees were being pulled across silver strings."

Sounder's bark is very important in the story. First, it is beautiful and it represents the hunt, the special ritual the man and dog— and sometimes the boy—share. It is also significant because it is the one sign of resistance shown to the sheriff and his deputies when they come to arrest the father. Finally, it is crucial because it disappears with the father and does not return until he does, despite the fact that there is no physical reason for Sounder to be unable to bark. When the father returns, so does Sounder's bark.

The dog's loyalty is expressed even further by the timing of his death. Although "by a dog's age, Sounder is past dying time," Sounder lives until his master returns, and until his master dies. Then Sounder "ain't got no spirit left for living," and dies, too.

Thinking about the characters

- What are some of the ways being able to read changes the boy's life?
- Do you think the father is right or wrong to steal the ham and sausages? What would you have done if you were in his shoes?
- Why do you think the mother is so accepting of her hard life? What, if anything, do you think she can do to change it?
- Why do you think Sounder doesn't bark until his master returns?

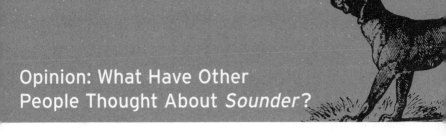
It's a winner!

Sounder is a winner—a Newbery Medal winner, that is. William H. Armstrong won the 1970 Newbery Medal for *Sounder.* The Newbery is a very prestigious honor: It is given annually by the children's librarians of the American Library Association to the author of "the most distinguished contribution to American literature for children" published during the preceding year. Look at your copy of *Sounder* and you may see the medal printed in gold on the cover.

In his Newbery acceptance speech, Armstrong said that up until the call came informing him of the award, the word *Newbery* meant something entirely different to him. It was the name of a store in the town where he had grown up that carried the toys of a boy's dreams. He never got most of the toys he saw there; he had to go home and make his own. "But tonight it is real," he said of the award. "The boy will not have to go home and hammer the Newbery Award out of the top of a Campbell Soup can."

In addition to being the recipient of the Newbery and other prestigious awards, the book, which has been in print for more than thirty years, has been translated into twenty-eight languages. *Sounder* was also made into a movie that was nominated for an Academy Award® in 1972.

What's in a name?

Critics debate Armstrong's choice not to give any of his characters, except the dog, a name. Some critics believe that this literary device makes the book more universal, meaning that it could be the story of any poor family in any place at any time. One critic wrote, "The human characters' namelessness lends them a universality as oppressed people, while . . . authentic, detailed descriptions . . . assure their individuality."

Other critics argue that this namelessness has racist overtones. "Within the white world, deep-seated prejudice has long denied human individualization to the Black person," wrote one critic, saying that Armstrong's use of this device "raises the issue of white supremacy."

Armstrong himself defended his use of this literary device, saying he learned "the art of omission" from listening to his mother read Old Testament Bible stories, where characters' ages, as well as places and times, were left out or kept vague. About his characters in *Sounder,* Armstrong said, "With names they would have represented one family; without names, they became universal—representing all people who suffer privation and injustice, but through love, self-respect, devotion, and desire for improvement, make it in the world."

Authentic

Some critics felt that a white man should not have been telling the story of this black family. They felt that a white person could not accurately describe the life of a family of a different race. Other reviewers, and Armstrong himself, disagreed.

One critic responded to the charge of lack of authenticity in this way: "It is not necessary or desirable that writer or critic be restricted to what he knows from direct experience; otherwise no man could write about women, no middle-aged person could write about old age; no one at all could write about the past. . . ."

Armstrong himself wrote, "I was writing about people's hearts and feelings. There's no color to feeling. There's no color to heart. There are a lot of white people who have suffered indignities. . . . And there are a lot of black people who have done the same thing."

Too frightening?

At least one critic even wondered whether this was, in fact, a book for children. When *Sounder* was published in 1969, a book reviewer for *The New York Times* wrote, "I am not sure children should read this book. If so, perhaps parents should loiter nearby, ready to enforce their child's revulsion from violence so truly and so well described." This critic felt that the violence was so well described it was frightening, perhaps too frightening for a child to read without a parent nearby.

Thinking about what others think about *Sounder*

- Do you think *Sounder* seems like an award-winning book? What other Newbery Medal–winning books have you read? How does *Sounder* compare?
- Do you agree with Armstrong's choice not to give his human characters names? Why or why not?
- Do you think authors should only be allowed to write from their own personal lives and experiences? Why or why not?
- Do you think *Sounder* is a book for children or adults or both? Why?

Glossary

Here are some words that may have been new to you in *Sounder*. Understanding these words will make it easier to read the novel.

addled mixed up or confused

animosity a strong dislike for someone

bramble a thorny bush or shrub

carcass the body of a dead animal

chitlins the small intestines of a pig, fried as food

chute a narrow, tilted passage down which things can slide, be pushed, or dropped

cistern a reservoir or tank for storing water

compulsion an irresistible urge to do something

conjure to make something happen by magic or sorcery

constrained held back; restrained

crockery pottery that you use for food, for example, cups and dishes

damper a movable plate in the smoke pipe of a wood stove that controls the draft

famished very hungry

gaunt very thin and bony

gingham checked cotton cloth

grub hoe a tool used to dig up roots

gyrations circular movements

inhuman cruel and brutal

intoxication great excitement or enthusiasm

malicious shown or done from a desire to hurt someone

mange a skin disease of dogs and other mammals

moccasin a water moccasin, a kind of poisonous snake

mongrel a dog that is a mixture of different breeds

orneriness stubbornness or meanness

pallet a small, narrow, hard bed

peddle to travel around selling things

persimmon an orange-red fruit that is shaped like a plum and
   is sweet and soft when ripe

plaintive sad and mournful

poultice a soft, moist, and often warm mass applied to sores
   and other injuries

quarry a place where stone, slate, or limestone is dug from the
   ground

quiver to tremble or vibrate

remote faraway, isolated, or distant

rivulet a small stream or brook

sanctuary a place of safety and protection

scrapple a hardened mush of ground pork and cornmeal that is sliced and fried

sharecropper a farmer who lives and works on land that belongs to someone else. Instead of using money to pay rent, a sharecropper agrees to give a certain amount of the crop to the landowner.

smokehouse an enclosed place where meat and fish are smoked and cured

sowbelly salt pork from the belly of a hog

sustain to keep something going

ticking cloth used to make pillows and mattresses

Although William H. Armstrong described himself as a teacher and not a writer, he was the author of more than fifteen books. And, although he didn't publish his first book until he was forty-two years old, he had been a writer when he was in high school and college. In fact, he nearly chose a career as a journalist.

Armstrong often recalled a story he wrote in high school, "Not Even with Wings," about a boy watching from his wheelchair as his pet cat climbed a tree outside his window and destroyed a nest of baby birds. It was so good and so original that neither his teacher nor the head of the English department believed Armstrong had written the story; they thought he must have copied it from somewhere. But he hadn't. He eventually went on to publish a revised version of the story in his college literary magazine, of which he was the editor, and sent copies to the two doubters. "Beautiful letters came from each," he said.

Despite being able to write and being drawn to writing at a young age, Armstrong put aside writing for nearly twenty years after graduating from college. "I enjoyed teaching so much, building my house with my own hands . . . reading to my children and helping my wife care for them that any thought of writing disappeared from my life." Then, in 1950, the headmaster and director of studies at Kent School asked him to write a book on how to study. Although reluctant at first, Armstrong eventually agreed, and he finished his first book, *Study Is Hard Work,* in 1953. It was published three years later.

Although Armstrong kept teaching—and building and farming and reading and raising children—he resumed his writing life. He described his writing routine as follows: "Early in the morning is my time to write. From 4 A.M. until 7 A.M. There is something very satisfactory about having one big job done before breakfast—like back on the farm with the milking before breakfast.

"I write with a pencil on a lined tablet. . . . I'm afraid a typewriter would somehow rob me of my own particular feeling."

Armstrong also recalled how he started his books: "Most of my books begin with an idea that I take inside [me] and keep there for a long time before I write a single word. It gets into my blood and is filtered through my heart until it is a part of me. *Sounder* . . . was filtered through my heart about four years before [I did] any writing except a few notes on 3″ × 5″ cards."

While the subjects, genres, and intended audiences of his books vary, Armstrong almost always wrote about the same themes: the importance of hard work, education, religious faith, and respect for nature.

For aspiring writers

Armstrong once said, "In speaking to young people who ask me how to start to become a writer, I say to them—dot your *i*'s and cross your *t*'s. Be proud of your schoolwork." After all, it was praise of a neat homework assignment in sixth grade that inspired Armstrong to achieve, to strive for excellence. But Armstrong's advice doesn't end there. He goes on to say:

> To that advice I add a second . . . thing to do: Read all the books you can. . . . Visiting elementary schools today brings a lump to my throat. I remember the scarcity of books that surrounded my early years (a short shelf in each classroom, a place for not more than a dozen books). I tell my audiences . . . that if I had by some magic been transported to such a library when I was their age, I wouldn't have gone home when school was out. I would have been reading until the last door was locked against me.

Armstrong has a very concrete example of how reading books can turn into writing books. The first book he owned was *Abraham Lincoln* by Lord Charnwood. It cost $1.65, and he earned the money to pay for it by digging sassafras sprouts for five cents an hour. He went on to collect hundreds of books about Lincoln and to write a highly praised book about this subject, *The Education of Abraham.*

So, Armstrong advises, be a conscientious student and read. "These things you do now in order to get ready to write your book twenty, thirty, forty years from now."

You Be the Author!

• **Share a story!:** As William Armstrong tells you in the introduction to *Sounder*, he wrote this book based on a story he had heard as a child. Armstrong didn't simply retell the story as he had heard it, he took what had he heard and used it as the skeleton of the story, then he fleshed it out, and made it his own as well as the teacher's who told it.

Listen to the stories people tell you—parents, siblings, grandparents, cousins, friends, teachers—and think about one that you might like to add to and make your own. Then, write your story. Be sure to share a copy with the person whose story started your own.

• **Epilogue:** Armstrong wrote two sequels to *Sounder*. Write a short story telling what you think happened to the boy when he grew up. What do you think his life was like?

• **Leaving out:** Practice "the art of omission," as Armstrong did. Find a short story in which names, ages, and locations are specific. Then, try rewriting it by leaving these specifics out. How does it change the story? You might even want to try writing your own story using this literary device.

• **A different point of view:** *Sounder* is told from the point of view of the boy. How do you think the story would be told differently from the mother's, the father's, or even the sheriff's point of view? Choose another character from the book and write a brief retelling of the story from that character's point of view.

• **A sense of place:** Armstrong's descriptive use of language helped establish the bleak setting in *Sounder.* You can practice establishing setting in a story by writing about the places you know best. Write about where you live, where you go to school, or even where you play ball. Use telling details to put the reader right where you want him! (You might even want to show what you write to someone who knows the area and see if she can guess the place you're writing about.)

Activities

• **Feed the hungry:** The family in *Sounder* is poor and often hungry. While you can't do anything to help the fictional family, you can do something to help feed poor people closer to home. You might want to organize a group of family members and friends to collect food for a soup kitchen or food pantry in your neighborhood.

If you cannot locate a need near home, find the name of one of the many national or international organizations whose goal is to feed people, and do some research on how you can help. Some groups that fight hunger are the United Nations' World Food Organization, America's Second Harvest, and Meals on Wheels.

• **Looking at a way of life:** In *Sounder,* the boy and his family are sharecroppers—tenant farmers who pay a share of their crop to the landowner for rent. This was how many Southern black people—and some white people—barely made a living after slavery was abolished. Research sharecropping to find out more about the way the boy and his family lived. You can get a better "picture" by checking out the University of Illinois Web site of sharecropping photos at www.english.uiuc.edu/maps/poets/a_f/brown/photos.htm. Think about how sharecropping compared with slavery: Was it a better way of life? Why or why not?

• **Lost dog:** Reread the author's description of Sounder early in the first chapter of the book. Research what a Georgia redbone hound and a bulldog look like. Then, make a "lost dog" poster for Sounder. In addition, you might want to write a newspaper advertisement describing the lost dog and asking for its return.

• **Letter to the editor:** Imagine you are a friend of the boy's family and have just heard the sentence the father has been given for stealing the ham and sausages. Write a letter to the editor of the local paper explaining what you think of the sentence.

• **Another faithful dog:** Armstrong explains that a teacher told him the story of Sounder after recounting the story of Odysseus's faithful dog, Argus. Read a retelling of the *Odyssey* (see Related Reading), then choose a part of the story—it could be about Argus or another character in the book—to tell to someone you know.

• **Listen to the music:** The boy's mother gave herself courage and comfort by singing and humming songs known as spirituals. Research these black religious folk songs to find out more about them, then borrow a tape or CD from the library and listen to the music that was an important part of the family's life in *Sounder*. You can find some good background information on these spirituals at www.negrospirituals.com.

• **Bible stories:** Read the Bible stories that the boy loved to hear his mother tell (the stories of Joseph and Abraham were the boy's favorites). Pay attention to what Armstrong describes as "the art of omission" in these stories. Ask yourself if you, too, can easily put yourself into these stories the way Armstrong says he did as a child, the way the boy in the book does.

• **Winning ways:** William H. Armstrong won the 1970 Newbery Medal for *Sounder.* Read one or two other Newbery-winning books and think about what it takes to be a winner. Some recent Newbery Medal books are:

Crispin: The Cross of Lead by Avi (2003 winner)
A Single Shard by Linda Sue Park (2002)
A Year Down Yonder by Richard Peck (2001)
Bud, Not Buddy by Christopher Paul Curtis (2000)
Holes by Louis Sachar (1999)
Out of the Dust by Karen Hesse (1998)
The View from Saturday by E. L. Konigsburg (1997)
The Midwife's Apprentice by Karen Cushman (1996)
Walk Two Moons by Sharon Creech (1995)
The Giver by Lois Lowry (1994)
Missing May by Cynthia Rylant (1993)

• **Get a library card!:** If you don't already have a library card, go get one and use it. Librarians will help you find whatever kind of book you're looking for—funny, sad, scary—and even make some good suggestions if you tell them what kinds of books you like.

Related Reading

***Sounder* sequels by William H. Armstrong**

Sour Land (1971)

The MacLeod Place (1972)

Other books by William H. Armstrong—fiction

Joanna's Miracle (1977)

The Mills of God (1973)

The Tale of Tawny and Dingo (1979)

Other books by William H. Armstrong—nonfiction

Barefoot in the Grass: The Story of Grandma Moses (1970)

The Education of Abraham Lincoln (1974)

Hadassah: Esther the Orphan Queen (1972)

My Animals (1974)

Tools of Thinking: A Self-Help Workbook for Students in Grades 5–9 (1968)

Books about African Americans—historical fiction

Black Angels by Rita Murphy

Color Me Dark: The Diary of Nellie Lee Love: The Great Migration North, Chicago, Illinois, 1919 (Dear America series) by Patricia C. McKissack

Dust of the Earth by Donna L. Hess

Forty Acres and Maybe a Mule by Harriet Gillem Robinet

The Forty-Acre Swindle by Dave and Neta Jackson

I Thought My Soul Would Rise and Fly: The Diary of Patsy, A Freed Girl (Dear America series) by Joyce Hansen

Jip: His Story by Katherine Paterson

Ludell by Brenda Wilkinson

Roll of Thunder, Hear My Cry by Mildred D. Taylor (this is the second in a series that also includes, in order, *The Land, Song of the Trees,* and *Let the Circle Be Unbroken*)

The Watsons Go to Birmingham—1963 by Christopher Paul Curtis

Books about African Americans—nonfiction

The Civil Rights Movement in America from 1865 to the Present by Patricia and Fredrick McKissack

Many Thousands Gone: African Americans from Slavery to Freedom by Virginia Hamilton

No More! Stories and Songs of Slave Resistance by Doreen Rapaport

Osceola: Memories of a Sharecropper's Daughter collected and edited by Alan Govenar

Slave Spirituals and the Jubilee Singers by Michael L. Cooper

Walk Together Children: Black American Spirituals by Ashley Bryan

Dog books—fiction

Because of Winn-Dixie by Kate DiCamillo

The Call of the Wild by Jack London

Love That Dog by Sharon Creech

Old Yeller by Fred Gipson

Shiloh by Phyllis Reynolds Naylor

Stone Fox by John Reynolds Gardiner

Where the Red Fern Grows by Wilson Rawls

White Fang by Jack London

Dog books—nonfiction

The Complete Dog Book for Kids by American Kennel Club Staff

Dog by Juliet Clutton-Brock

Understanding Man's Best Friend: Why Dogs Look and Act the Way They Do by Ann Squire

Other

The Wanderings of Odysseus: The Story of The Odyssey by Rosemary Sutcliff

Movies

Sounder is available on VHS.

Bibliography

Books

Armstrong, William H. *Sounder.* New York: Harper & Row, 1969.

Armstrong, William H. *Through Troubled Waters.* New York: Harper & Brothers, 1957.

Authors and Artists for Young Adults. Volumes 7–26. Detroit: The Gale Group, Inc., 1992–1999.

Children's Literature Review. Volume 1. Detroit: The Gale Group, Inc., 1976.

St. James Guide to Young Adult Writers. 2nd edition. Detroit: The Gale Group, Inc./St. James Press, 1999.

Something About the Author. Volume 4. Detroit: The Gale Group, Inc., 1973.

Something About the Author. Volume 111. Detroit: The Gale Group, Inc., 2000.

Something About the Author Autobiography Series. Volume 7. Detroit: The Gale Group, Inc., 1988.

Third Book of Junior Authors. New York: H. W. Wilson Co., 1972.

Newspapers and magazines

Horn Book Magazine, August 1970, pp. 352–358.

The New York Times, April 25, 1999, p. 47.

The New York Times Book Review, October 26, 1969, p. 42.

Web sites

Contemporary Authors Online, Gale, 2002:
www.galenet.com/servlet/BioRC

Educational Paperback Association:
www.edupaperback.org/authorbios/Armstrong_William.html